MY
FAVORITE
DEVOTIONAL
STORIES

MY
FAVORITE
DEVOTIONAL
STORIES

PAUL BUCHHEIMER

Kravitz & Sons

INNOVATORS IN PUBLISHING, MARKETING AND ADVERTISING

Kravitz and Sons LLC
204 E Arlington Blvd. Suite B
Greenville, NC 27858

Published by Kravitz and Sons LLC.

ISBN: 979-8-89639-663-5 (sc)
ISBN: 979-8-89639-662-8 (e)

Library of Congress Control Number: 2026907847

This book is dedicated to:

- my wife and partner in ministry for 56 years, Peggy
- my three children, Matt, Joy, and Brooke
- my seven grandchildren, Austin, Cody, Tianna, Kyle, Ben, Cooper, and Charles.
- my father, Paul, who served in ministry for 57 years
- my mother, Marian, and my siblings, Susan and Richard

All the Bible references I use in this book are taken from The <u>Holy Bible, New International Version,</u> Copyright 1973, 1978, 1984, by International Bible Society, Zondervan.

Table of Contents

My Favorite Devotional Stories

<u>By: Paul Buchheimer</u>

Excerpt: *My Favorite Devotional Stories transforms everyday moments into meaningful reflections of faith. With warmth and authenticity, Paul Buchheimer shares heartfelt wisdom and spiritual insight in a voice that feels like a trusted friend, offering encouragement, hope, and inspiration for daily life.*

A Heartfelt Devotional That Inspires and Uplifts

From the very first pages of *My Favorite Devotional Stories*, Paul Buchheimer invites readers into a deeply personal yet universally relatable spiritual journey. Growing up as a pastor's son, Buchheimer's reflections are rooted in a lifetime of real-world faith experiences rather than abstract theology, which makes each devotional feel authentic, sincere, and immediately applicable. Whether you are just beginning your spiritual walk or have been on the path for years, the stories shared here resonate with emotional depth and a grounded sense of hope.

One of the book's greatest strengths is its ability to take everyday encounters and ordinary moments and reveal the extraordinary ways God's presence can be seen within them. Each entry is crafted with clarity and warmth, making complex spiritual truths accessible without ever diluting their significance. The author's engaging voice feels less like a distant preacher and more like a trusted friend sharing encouragement over coffee; this creates an inviting reading experience that draws you back day after day.

What sets this devotional apart is how it balances heartfelt storytelling with practical insight. Buchheimer does not merely recount his experiences; he reflects on them in ways that challenge the reader to consider the deeper implications of faith in everyday life. Across the chapters, themes of grace, perseverance, humility, and gratitude emerge naturally without seeming forced or overly didactic. Each story subtly nudges the reader to look inward, to recognize God's work in their own life, and to respond with gratitude and renewed purpose.

The structure of the book makes it perfect for both daily devotional use and thoughtful, reflective reading. Each story stands on its own, allowing readers to pause and ponder a single lesson or to read several entries in one sitting for a broader perspective. The tone throughout is gracious and encouraging, inviting readers not only to reflect on their spiritual journey but also to grow in depth and compassion. This balance of inspiration and introspection elevates *My Favorite Devotional Stories* beyond a typical devotional collection; it becomes a meaningful resource for spiritual growth.

Rating: ★ ★ ★ ★ ★ (5/5)

My Favorite Devotional Stories deserves a full 5 out of 5 stars because it delivers exactly what readers of devotional and inspirational literature seek: heartfelt wisdom, accessible spiritual insight, and authentic encouragement grounded in real-life experience. Paul Buchheimer's gift for transforming ordinary moments into meaningful reflections of faith allows the book to connect with a broad audience, from those beginning their spiritual journey to longtime believers looking for renewed perspective. This devotional also merits a strong presence in physical bookstores, as it fills an important space within the Christian inspirational and devotional genre. Its relatable storytelling and thoughtful reflections make it ideal for placement in sections dedicated to faith, personal growth, and daily devotionals, offering readers a sincere and uplifting resource that stands out for its warmth, depth, and spiritual nourishment.

INTRODUCTION
THE IMPACT OF A GOOD STORY

I remember sitting in church one morning and watching two teenage boys trying to keep awake and control themselves. They were paying absolutely no attention to the pastor's preaching. But then, when the pastor started to tell a story, they stopped their fooling around and very intently listened to every word of the story. However, when the story ended, they returned to their previous behavior and started to poke one another. This incident, which I'm sure is repeated in churches, classrooms, and lecture halls worldwide, really made me appreciate the impact a good storyteller can have on an audience.

I appreciate that I have had the opportunity to hear over the years. There are many more stories that I could tell, but I hope you will enjoy the ones that I have chosen. We are told that we forget 95% of what we hear after 72 hours. I will remember many of the stories I have written in this book for the rest of my life. I hope that at least some of these stories will get past at least the 72-hour test for you. But more importantly, I hope to communicate the critical message that the only way to be saved is through Jesus Christ. In John 11:26, Jesus tells us that "I am the resurrection. If anyone believes in Me, even though he dies, he will LIVE."

JANE HAMPTON

Lake Weir High School is a large public high school in Candler, Florida. I assume that the student body's makeup today is not that much different than when I taught there from 1982 until 1993. About forty percent of the students were African American, another forty percent Hispanic mostly from the New York City area, and the remaining twenty percent were rednecks from the surrounding countryside. It made for an interesting school environment.

I was a math teacher. My specialty and real love was geometry, but I also taught algebra. In 1990 one of the classes I was assigned was teaching algebra to juniors and seniors. Needless to say, this class would not have ever been mistaken for a calculus class. It was pretty apparent that none of these students wanted to be there. They all had one thing in common--they didn't like math. That was my challenge.

Teachers will tell you that even though they are professional and treat all their students with respect, there are some students each year who stand out from the others. You will have some students you don't always like, and others you will enjoy having in class and develop a special bond with them. For me, Jane Hampton was such a student. She was bright and alert, and funny. She seemed to enjoy life and was very popular. Even though she made it clear from the beginning that she hated math, she still made the best of things and kept a positive attitude. Right from the start, we connected. We often kidded with each other and always found something to talk about. I looked forward to having Jane in class each day.

As the year went on, a wonderful thing happened. Jane began to improve in math and even reluctantly admitted at times that "math wasn't so bad after all." In fact, by the end of the year, Jane was one of the best students in class and was earning good grades on tests and quizzes. Naturally, I felt terrific about this and started to pat myself on the back for my excellent teaching.

On the last day of class, Jane wrote me a note and told me how much she enjoyed the course and how much I had meant to her. She hoped that I would be her teacher again next year for geometry. If not, she wrote, she would come by often and say hi, and we could talk.

That next fall, Jane was not assigned to my class, and even though her geometry class was right next door to mine, we did not see each other very often. She was busy with her friends and new schedule, and I had new students to worry about. At the end of the following year, however, Jane did come by and tell me that she was excited about graduating and would give me one of her senior class pictures.

Because Lake Weir High School was located in the country, virtually all students had to ride school buses daily. When they got old enough, most would buy a car or a truck to drive themselves to school. This also meant that many would drive great distances during the weekends to meet with their friends to party. I often dreaded opening my newspaper on Sunday mornings because I often read that some of my students had gotten into car accidents.

On the Sunday before graduation, sure enough, there was news that there had been a two-car collision and one of the fatalities was Jane Hampton. At Lake Weir High School, it just so happened there were two Jane Hamptons. Besides the Jane I taught algebra, there was also the other Jane I had also taught. She was a tall girl who pitched for the softball team that year. For the rest of the day and all night, I did not know which Jane had been killed. Of course, it bothered me that either girl could have been the one who had died, but I was especially close to the algebra Jane.

I'll never forget the scene that followed the next morning. I was walking on the sidewalk leading to the school's side door when suddenly the door opened and out came Jane Hampton. It was the tall softball pitcher. It was at that moment that I suddenly realized something very sobering. I did not know where the other Jane Hampton was or where she would be for the rest of eternity. I had spent so much time with

Jane, talking about so many different things, but did I ever witness to her about Jesus? Sure I felt very successful about her math progress, but what difference did it make now?

I felt tremendous guilt at that moment, and I still carry that guilt around today. Where will Jane spend the rest of eternity? Could I have made a difference?

At the funeral one of Jane's best friends came up to me and gave me one of Jane's senior pictures. "This is for you. Jane talked about you a lot, and I know she had promised you one of these. I am sure she wanted you to have this."

I thought back to that feeling I had on the walkway when I realized that "my" Jane Hampton was gone. No matter how much she learned, only one thing now made a difference. It reminded me that the only knowledge that ever makes a difference in a person's life is the acceptance of Jesus Christ as the sacrifice for the punishment of our sins. Did Jane know that?

From that day on, I decided that in every class I teach, at some time or another, I would tell my students that truth. In Christian schools, of course, it would be the natural thing to do quite often. But even in public school classrooms, I will at least end the year with that message. Our salvation through the blood of Jesus is far too important. The most crucial thing in a person's life is their relationship with Jesus Christ. In the end, nothing else will matter.

QUESTION TO CONSIDER:

How many people around you don't know or accept Jesus Christ as their savior? How many members of your own family, or people whom you care for very much, will not be in heaven even though you had plenty of time to share the message of salvation with them? If we genuinely love and care for them, why don't we give them the most important thing on earth, or at least try?

Lord, may the Holy Spirit open the hearts of those we love to accept a savior. Amen.

THE CIRCUS COMES TO TOWN

When I was a young boy my family was similar to my friends' families. My father was a minister in a small church, and Mom stayed home to take care of my brother, sister, and me. None of our neighbors or acquaintances had much money, indeed no different. I remember many days and nights when my parents would go into my dad's office and "emotionally discuss" how they could pay off the bills and still keep food on the table. There was no extra money for any spending that was outside of our budgeted necessities. Somehow God always provided us with our needs, if not our wants. The three of us knew how much our parents would have enjoyed being able to spend at least a little extra on us, but even for Christmas and our birthdays, coming up with any extra money was just not possible. I guess that is why one of my fondest memories occurred on the day when the circus came to town.

After my father read in the paper one morning that the circus would be set up in our small town for several performances, he excitedly exclaimed to my Mom that he wanted to take us to see the big top. She reminded him that we really could not afford it, but he could not be talked out of it.

"Come on kids," Father yelled as he burst into our bedroom that Saturday morning. "Today will be a special day you will never forget. We are going to the circus!" We were still half asleep and stunned, but it didn't take us long to leap out of our beds and start dancing around the bedroom. We had all seen a circus on television but we never thought that we would get to go to a real one.

The three of us dressed quickly and rushed into the kitchen to have our breakfast. We weren't the least bit hungry, but we knew Mom would insist that we had something. As we gulped down our juice and cereal, we couldn't hold back the anticipation of how much fun we would be having. Dad told us to slow down because the circus wouldn't open until early afternoon, but we didn't care. We were ready and wanted to leave right away. After cleaning up our rooms and waiting for what seemed to be forever, Dad finally told us that we could get into the car--it was time to leave.

As we drove to the outskirts of town, the three of us were excited! There would be clowns, acrobats, and of course, animals. Richard couldn't wait to see the real live lions and tigers. Susan was looking forward to seeing the trapeze artists way above the crowd. I just wanted to take in all of the sights and smells of an actual live event.

After what seemed like a very long drive, we parked on the dirt field, walked through the dusty and bumpy lot, and arrived quickly at the front gate.

There was a long line, but it moved quickly. In front of us was a man who had his three young children. They seemed even more excited than we were as they laughed and jumped up and down. I could see in the young man's face how proud he was to be able to bring such pleasure to his children's lives. He finally got to the ticket window and happily told the ticket taker that he needed tickets for one adult and three children. He pulled something out of his pocket along with his wallet. He gave the lady a coupon he had cut out of the newspaper.

"Here you are, madam. This coupon is good for free admission for my children."

"I'm sorry," the older woman who sold the tickets replied. "This coupon is only good for one child's admission. You still owe me four dollars for the other two children."

A look of panic swept over the father's face. This had caught him by complete surprise.

"Please, ma'am, let me see that coupon."

The ticket taker seemed annoyed that he would slow down all the people in the line to question her about this.

"Here you are, sir. You can see at the bottom of the coupon in fine print that it clearly states that this discount is only good for one child with an adult purchase. You still owe me another four dollars!"

She was right, and he now saw what he had overlooked before. What was he to do? He looked down at his young kids; they had no idea what was happening and that there might be a chance they would not get in. You could see on his face that he was at a total loss as to what to do. He simply did not have the additional four dollars.

He then leaned up close to the lady. "Oh please, can't you just make an exception this time and let the other two kids in?"

"Sir, there is nothing I can do. Now please, either pay the rest of the charge or get out of the line and let the next customer through. It's not my problem that you can't read. If I make an exception for you then I will have to do it for others in the line that are seeing this. Maybe next time, you will be more careful and learn not to try to cheat others out of what you owe."

Watching this scene unfold, I noticed my father doing a bizarre thing. He carefully took a five-dollar bill out of his pocket and threw it on the ground at his feet.

"Excuse me, sir," he said to the father in front of him. "When you took out your money you must have dropped this bill on the ground. Here, this is yours."

At first, the startled man began to deny that he had dropped the money, but then he suddenly caught on to what my father was doing. As he bent down to pick up the money, I saw the look on his face. It envisioned gratitude and relief at the same time.

"Thank you so much, sir," he said in a voice choked up with emotion. "Here you are, madam. Come on, kids, let's go to the circus."

Now that my dad no longer had enough money to pay for our admission, he motioned us to step out of the line and start to walk back to our car.

"Hey, where are we going?" my sister asked.

"Yeah, why aren't we going inside?" asked my brother.

My father couldn't answer them then, but I was older and knew what was going on. When we all got back into the car, nobody said a word. My sister and brother we so stunned and disappointed that they just looked out of the window.

As we continued on the drive home, I looked up at my Dad and couldn't help but notice tears in his eyes. At that moment, I never felt prouder to be his son. Dad was right. This certainly was a day I would never forget.

QUESTION TO CONSIDER:

What motivates you to do good works? Do you do something out of guilt or to earn the admiration or praise of others? Think of a time when you did something to help someone else without them even knowing about it.

Lord, may our good deeds be done out of love and not for our own rewards and glory. Amen.

BASEBALL SAVES A LIFE

As a teacher, you can sometimes plan events and field trips that interest you more than what interests the students. Teaching in Central Florida allowed me to plan an annual trip to see a spring training game. I knew that the students were excited just to get a day out of school, even if a baseball game did not interest them, so there was excitement as we loaded the bus and headed off to the game.

After four or five innings I could always count on most of the students to become bored and want the game to end, but some of us did watch the game and enjoy it. As we loaded back on the bus, not much was said.

Many years later, I received a surprising letter from a student who had attended the game. There was no way that I could have been prepared for what he had to write. Chuck started his letter by sharing with me how he remembered that game and how much it had changed his life.

Chuck shared how depressed and unhappy he was during that year in the eighth grade. His mother had gotten a divorce, and his new stepfather was abusive to him both physically and sexually. Chuck had reached a point where he could no longer take it and was on the verge of suicide. Then he went to the game. He was fascinated with something that he had never experienced in his life. There was something about the sport of baseball that captivated his interest. He discovered something that took him out of his misery and brought a new passion to him. He went home that night, started following the teams, and watched and listened to as many games as possible.

Chuck wrote that he went on to graduate from high school and college, married, and now had a family of his own. Baseball continued to be his escape in life and helped him cope with many problems and challenges. His love of baseball was passed on to his son, who grew very close, sharing their love of the sport.

He closed his letter by thanking me for taking him to the game that day and how it had saved his life from ending it all that year. I could never have guessed that in bringing pleasure to several other students and me that day, I made such a difference in a student's life.

QUESTION TO CONSIDER:

Have you ever stopped to think how many people you have positively and negatively influenced by words and actions?

Dear God, may you use me to make a positive difference in the lives of those people who I meet in my life.

MOTIVATION 1

In college football, even in some of the smaller schools, teams would have a traveling squad and an expanded home roster. Some players would practice with the team but dress out only for home games. Bobby Mason was such a player. He suited out and sat on the bench for only the home games. It wasn't worth the school's money for him to travel to away games when he would seldom get into the games at all.

The season had not been a good one for the Crusaders. They had won only two games and going into their last week, there was no chance of them making the playoffs. This definitely would be their last game of the season. As Coach Price sat behind his desk, trying to devise a plan that might work a miracle for his woeful eleven, he was surprised to see young Mason at his door.

"Come on in, kid," he barked. He called him kid because he wasn't even sure of this guy's name.

"Coach, I'm Bobby Mason, and I need to talk with you about something," the shy young man barely whispered to the imposing coach.

"Coach, I just got a phone call from home. It was my brother, and he told me that my father had just passed away."

"I'm so sorry to hear that." The coach's mood changed quickly as he stood up and approached the thin young man. "You must go home right away and be at your mother's side at a time like this. I certainly understand that you will miss our final game."

"That's what I wanted to talk to you, sir. I don't want to go home; I want to be with the team this Saturday."

The coach looked right into the boy's eyes and was insistent. "No, that would not be right. You must go home right away. Your family needs you to be there."

"Please, sir, I've thought it over, and I beg you to let me be with the team. I cannot let you and all of the other players down. I promise that as soon as the game ends, I will drive home and be with all of my family that night. The funeral will not be until Monday."

"Well, guy, I don't agree with you at all, but I can see that being at the game means so much to you at a time like this. Okay, you can be there with us this Saturday."

Just as the coach sat back down behind the big desk, the boy moved closer and summoned the courage to ask the coach for one more favor.

"Coach, I have one more thing to ask you. I understand that you don't know what I can do on the field, but it would mean an awful lot to me at this time if you would do me one huge favor. I would like to be in the starting lineup for this game."

The coach was surprised and looked down at his shoes for a long moment. Finally, he raised his head and replied, "Okay, kid, I will let you start."

The coach realized that his team was not very good anyway and that this last game was meaningless in terms of the win-lose record and the team's rankings. Besides, how much harm could this kid do just by starting and playing a few downs? The young man thanked the coach, quickly left the office, and ran back to his dorm room.

That Saturday afternoon, the players were shocked when they saw that Bobby Mason's name was down as a starting lineman. Nobody said anything, but the coach could tell that his team was wondering what was happening. Was the coach giving up?

On the opening kickoff, Bobby raced down the field shed two blockers, and slammed the ball carrier viciously to the ground. On the first play from the line of scrimmage, Bobby again tackled the runner for a five-yard loss. Play after play went the same way. Bobby was all over the field and was totally dominating the game.

The Crusaders pulled a big upset that day, and Bobby was certainly a big reason for the strong showing. His tremendous effort inspired all of the players to play their best.

After the game, the coach awarded the game b, and all the players cheered. The jubilant coach then asked Bobby to come to his office.

"Great game, Bobby," the coach congratulated the tired young man. "I never would have guessed that you could play like that. Today, kid, you played like an all-American. What got into you?"

"Coach, you never met my Dad, did you?"

"No, young man, I never did have the pleasure. But I'm sure he was a fine man."

"Coach, my Dad was blind, and today was the first time he ever got to see me play."

Do you ever wonder what you can accomplish if you put your mind to something and find the motivation to do your best? Jesus tells us in Matthew 19:26 that "with God, all things are possible."

How often do we not succeed because our lack of faith and effort let us down?

QUESTION TO CONSIDER:

What motivates you? What drives you to do your best? Is it money or success? What is important to us?

God, help us to live in this world and not of it. Amen.

TAKING CARE OF A PET BIRD

Mark 8:36: "What good is it for a man to gain the whole world, yet forfeit his soul? "

A man entered a pet store and told the clerk he wanted to buy a bird. "But not just any bird," he exclaimed. "I want the most expensive bird available-money is no object."

"Yes, sir," responded the pet shop salesman. "We just got in a scarce bird species, but it will be costly," the clerk warned. "The cost of this particular species will be $5,000."

"Wow! That is expensive! But like I said, money is no object. This bird will be a gift for my wife on our twenty-fifth anniversary, and this bird is what she wants. No other bird will do. She wants the bird as an investment that will increase in value over time."

"That's fine," replied the salesman. "But don't forget that you will need to purchase more than just the bird. You will need a top-of-the-line cage to keep her in."

"I see," answered the man. "Well, since I'm buying a great bird I want to buy the best cage I can to keep her in."

So the good husband paid five grand for the bird and another $200 for the cage and left to proudly show his wife her gift. But the next day he returned to the pet shop.

"Can you give me some advice?" the man requested. "My wife complained that her bird seemed bored and just sat on her perch all day. My wife wants a happy, active pet."

"Of course, your bird is bored. She has nothing to do all day just sitting in a plain, empty cage. You need to get her something that will occupy her time. I have just the thing."

The salesman, hoping to make even more money off of the poor confused husband, came back with a large box with a slide and a swing on the front panel.

"This is exactly what you need. It's the latest thing for birds. It's called the Birdie Gym. Put this together in her cage, and she will stay in good shape and be busy all day with the little exercise devices!"

"That makes sense," the man replied. So he purchased the Birdie Gym for only $79 and was off to set it up for the bird.

Two days later, the man returned to the shop once more. He seemed more confused than ever.

"So, how did your bird like the gym set?" asked the clerk.

"At first, she seemed to enjoy it," answered the man. "But after a short time, she lay down again and seemed to lose all interest in the gym equipment. She just doesn't seem to have any energy."

"I know exactly the problem, " the sales clerk answered. "There is probably too much light so the bird isn't getting enough sleep. I should have told you to buy a cover for the birdcage. Then she will be able to sleep during the day and at night."

"This is getting ridiculous," complained the frustrated bird owner. "I wish you had told me all this when I bought the bird. Now I am finding out how much owning a bird costs!"

"Sorry about that, sir, but I think with the cage cover we finally will have everything we need for your wife to enjoy her bird. Since you've been such a good customer, I will give you a special price on the cover."

"I appreciate that, but this better be the end of all this!" The dejected customer seemed broken down as he slinked out of the pet shop for what he hoped would be the last time. He didn't want even to estimate how much this gift for his wife had cost him.

Three days later, the bird owner violently pushed open the store door and stormed up to the front co,unter where he could no longer control himself.

"I have spent a fortune and wasted so much of my time in your store and now look at what has happened!" he screamed. "The bird is dead!"

The clerk tried to bring some peace to the situation. "Sir, please calm down. I'm sure we can figure this out. Now for starters, what have you been feeding her?"

The astonished owner looked at the clerk in a very peculiar way. "What do you mean feeding her? You never told me that I had to feed her!"

So many times, we get caught up in the many minor details of our lives that we forget the most important things. The only fact in our lives that will make a difference for us through all eternity is whether we accept Jesus Christ as our savior. Without God's grace and mercy that He gave us when he sent His son, Jesus Christ, through his death and resurrection, anything and everything we obtain and accomplish here on earth is meaningless. Just like the poor bird owner, we find ourselves so caught up in all of the other day-by-day needs, possessions, and worries that we overlook the one thing that counts.

QUESTION TO CONSIDER:

We all know what we need in life to survive—food, water, shelter, and love. Why do we forget about our need for forgiveness from the sins we commit every day?

Lord, I know I can't live without your grace and mercy daily. Without you, all life would cease to exist. Amen.

MOTHER'S DAY

"Really? This is just my luck! Here I am swamped with appointments, clients to meet, paperwork all over the place, and now this. I've got to stand here and wait while some little ragamuffin counts out pennies?"

The well-dressed businessman of the world was very much in a rush as he waited in line to order some flowers for his mother. He really couldn't spare the time for this stop. However, tomorrow was Mother's Day, and he had to do something for his mother. Having some flowers wired to her seemed like the easiest thing to do at this late date.

"Count out the right amount, get your cheap little bunch of flowers, and get out of my way," said Mr. Businessman under his breath.

Finally, the young boy had finished counting and pushed all of the coins across the counter to the owner of the floral shop.

"I'm sorry young man, but you are still about three dollars short, and this is the least expensive flower arrangement I have."

The little guy looked down at his feet and didn't know what to say or do.

"Come on already," barked the salesman. "I'm in a hurry and can't wait any longer. How much does the kid owe you?"

"He's three dollars and forty-nine cents short," said the florist.

"Just add it to my bill. I want to order some flowers to be delivered to my mother."

"Gee, thanks, mister," the little boy said as he looked up at the man. "Don't even think about it, kid. It's no big deal."

It wasn't a big deal to the wealthy salesman, and if it would get him out of there and on his way, it was well worth it to him. Besides, being able to help this little boy felt kind of satisfying.

The little boy grabbed the flower arrangement and rushed out of the door. "Thanks again, mister."

The businessman moved up to the counter and asked the florist to pick something nice and send it to his mother. After giving the address and his credit card, he was given a blank note to sign and attach to the flowers. He didn't know what to write because he had rarely visited or seen his mother in the past year. He just scribbled Love, John, under the accompanying card's verse, which he didn't even bother to read.

There, he thought, I can get on to my next appointment now that's done for another year. However, as he rushed out the door, he thought about his mother. Ever since he had put her in the nursing home, he had only visited her once and never talked to her on the phone. After Dad died, Mom went downhill quickly. He suspected she had already been slipping before that, but Dad did a lot to cover up for her. Seeing her at the home in the condition she was in really kind of de- pressed him, so he never went over there again. Besides, his business had picked up, and he didn't have much free time anyway.

As he got into his car and started driving slowly down the street, he noticed the same little boy in the flower shop walking quickly on the sidewalk. It was a freezing, windy day, and the boy had only a light jacket. He pulled over to the curb and rolled down the window.

"Hey, kid, do you want a ride?"

"No, thanks, I'm okay," replied the boy. The man could see that the boy was shaking and was feeling the effects of the strong wind on his face.

"No, come on. I'm going the same way you are, and it's no trouble for me to give you a lift. Jump in."

The boy looked up and agreed to get in the car. As the boy closed the door, the man saw that the little guy's hands were red and shaking badly.

After a minute of silence, the man asked, "How far are you going?"

"Oh, it's not too much farther," answered the boy. As the two rode on through the crowded streets, they were quiet and looked at all the traffic and the busy sidewalks. The driver asked the boy what his name was, and when the lad told him his name was John, the man laughed and said that was also his name.

Finally, the young passenger asked the man a question. "Are you going to see your mother? Where are the flowers you bought her?"

"No, my mother lives about an hour away, and I'm swamped. I had the florist send the flowers to her. I'll give her a call later tomorrow and make sure she got my gift."

Voicing those words brought on feelings of guilt; his attempt to honor his mother on Mother's Day now seemed to be empty and hollow.

Suddenly the little boy again broke the silence. "You can take the next turn to the right. It's only a little bit farther."

Just a couple of blocks later, the boy told the man that he could pull up on the right and stop at the side of the street. "This is where I'm getting out."

The man looked around and was very puzzled. "Son, you must be mixed up. There are no houses around here. There's just this little cemetery."

"Yes, this is the right place. I'm taking the flowers to put on my mother's grave. She died last year, and now I live in a foster home. My Dad left me when I was very young, and she was the only family I had. Now I try to see her as often as I can. I certainly wanted to bring her a gift for Mother's Day."

As little Johnny jumped out of the car, he thanked the man and ran off into the cemetery. John just sat very still for a long time. He felt tears welling up in his eyes, and a feeling of emptiness overcame him. Suddenly he turned the car around right in the middle of traffic and sped back to the florist.

"Ma'am, is it too late for me to change my order? I don't want to send those flowers. I want to pick them up here and take them myself to my mother."

"I'm sorry, sir, but I've already sent out the order."

"Well, then never mind. Please give me the most beautiful arrangement you have, and she'll get to have two bouquets this year. And please hurry. I need to see her right away!"

As John left the flower shop for the second time, suddenly the wind didn't feel so cold anymore.

God has blessed our lives with those who we love and love us. How often do we take them for granted and not appreciate how much they mean to us? We know that nothing on earth lasts forever, and our time with our loved ones is precious and will someday be gone.

QUESTION TO CONSIDER:

Do you often take for granted those who love you? Do you neglect to tell them how much you love them?

Father in heaven, you've blessed us with so many family and friends who care about us. May we appreciate their love for us every day and show them how much we care. Amen.

WATCHING THE BIG GAME

Having season tickets to our local hockey team, The Stars has been a source of enjoyment for my wife and me for many years now. The only problem is when there is a schedule conflict and we can't use our tickets for that night. Such a conflict did come up for us last October. We had to choose between attending the hockey game and watching our favorite baseball team play in game 7 of their playoff run on television. We decided we could record the game on our DVR and watch it when we returned from the hockey game.

As we watched the hockey game, we kept wondering how the baseball game was going. Finally, the Stars' game ended, and we rushed home to see how the baseball game had turned out. As soon as we opened the door to our house, I turned on the television and deliberately went right to the recorded shows and turned on the beginning of the baseball game.

The two teams were engaged in a tight battle, and the lead went back and forth. Finally, in the eighth inning, the other team seemed to break the game open with a three-run outburst. Now our team was down to their final chance. I could see that my wife was very anxious as she prayed for a final rally. Sure enough, they scored the tying run, and then a homerun topped off the comeback. Our team had mounted an exciting comeback and was going to move on to the World Series.

After I turned off the set, my wife asked me how I could stay so calm and not get so scared and worried about the outcome of the game.

"You just seemed so relaxed and confident that our team would win, even when things looked the worst. I was so afraid that the outcome would not be good for us. I was on pins and needles the whole time, but you never even seemed worried that our team might lose. How were you able to stay so calm?"

"It was very easy. You see, during the hockey game, I went to the restroom. When I returned to my seat, some,e loudmouth yelled to everyone around him that our team had just won their game. So I already knew the game's outcome and didn't worry about what might happen. I knew all along that the results of the game would be a victory for our team."

Do you see how this example can apply to us and our lives? God has already promised that, because He sent a Savior who defeated sin and eternal damnation, we don't need to worry or be anxious about what will happen to us when we die. We already know how things will work out in the end.

Why do we get so worried and uptight about so many things? Despite all the hardships, disappointments, and grief we experience in our lives, everything will work out. We are winners; nothing here on earth can take away our salvation. We don't need to stress what others think about us or how successful and popular we are. Everything in our life is temporal--only our future in Heaven with God will never go away.

So the next time you find yourself worried sick about money, your job, or your future, stop for a minute and put it all in perspective. Don't let Satan bring you down and spoil things for you. God has won the victory for us; we should rejoice and be thankful daily. God has made us winners for all eternity. Find comfort in that promise.

QUESTION TO CONSIDER:

Have you ever lost sleep and peace because you worried over something, only to discover later that you didn't need to worry about it?

Lord, we can turn our problems and worries over to You. In the end, help us trust

SCORING THE WINNING RUN

Maybe it wasn't such a big thing for everyone else. Still, to the 25 players and coaches, the Upstate Semi-Professional League's championship game meant everything this August afternoon. The Ballston Scotties and the Saratoga Navy Vets had each won in the playoff rounds and now had earned the right to vie for the biggest prize-a championship.

The Scotties were primarily a young squad made up of recent high school graduates and several college players home for the summer. The Navy Vets were more of an experienced team. The Saratoga nine even had a former minor leaguer or two and several players who were in their forties. Johnny Gobels had even made it to triple-A but threw out his arm and could hardly reach first base from his third base position.

The Semi-pro league paid the players a few dollars for each game, but nobody played for the money. It cost many players more in gas money than they could earn playing. It was simply a love of the game. Being able to put on a uniform, throw a ball and swing a bat, and kid around with teammates was the ultimate source of joy for these guys. But once the game started, it was all business.

It was windy and rather cold for an August afternoon. The twenty or thirty spectators, most loyal and faithful wives and children of the players, bundled together in the worn-down bleachers on the first base side. They knew how much this game meant to their beloved and just hoped their dads or husbands would not get hurt and could walk back to the car without much pain and agony.

It was apparent right from the first pitch that both teams were well-matched. The two pitchers didn't throw very hard, but they did throw strikes, and the batters were up there to swing the bats, not to wait for walks. Between the booted ground balls and the misjudged fly balls, there were enough good plays to keep the game moving. Going into the bottom of the ninth the game was tied at six, and now the Saratoga Navy Vets were in a position to win it all as they batted in the bottom of the ninth. After two quick outs, the fate of the Vets rested on the shoulders of their weak hitting shortstop, Dave "Jitters" Bancroft. Dave earned his nickname by getting nervous whenever anyone hit a groundball at him. As he got set in the batter's box and took his stance, there didn't seem to be much hope that the .143-hitting Jitters would be able to avoid an extra-inning contest.

But suddenly and very surprisingly, with a 1 and 2 count, Jitters stepped into a pitch that was right down the middle and drove the ball to deep right-center field. Since there were no fences in the outfield, the ball rolled past the outfielders and went all the way to a children's playground.

Finally, the right fielder reached the baseball and relayed it to the second baseman. The relay man turned quickly and threw the ball as hard as he could toward home plate. Meanwhile, Jitters had rounded third, slipped, but then got up and raced toward home. It was going to be close-a real bang bang play! Jitters slid awkwardly and touched the plate with his left hand just as the catcher caught the ball and tagged at the runner. Suddenly it became hushed. The umpire finally made his call after a very long time. "The runner is out!"

All of the players and fans were stunned. It was undeniable that Jitters had beaten the tag. Then the outrage began. Fans were screaming and throwing things onto the field. The Navy Vets manager, Benny Fasulo, had to be restrained by his players. How could this be possible?

The three umpires gathered by the pitching mound and held their arms up, asking for silence. When the crowd finally quieted, the base umpire was ready to clarify the call.

"The runner was out; he yelled so that all could hear, "Not because the throw home beat him, but because he missed first base. " In all of the action, Jitters had gotten so excited that he never touched first base.

The Scotties scored seven runs in the top of the tenth to bring home the trophy to Ballston Spa.

Unfortunately, many people believe that they can earn their way into heaven. They live a good life and try to be the best they can be. But they forget to touch first base. We miss the essential part of our lives if we haven't accepted Jesus Christ as our savior and received his merciful gift of forgiveness. Whatever else we do won't count when judgment day arrives if we forgot to touch first base.

QUESTION TO CONSIDER:

Why do we forget all about the essentials of life each day? Some day we might look back on our lives and realize that we missed out on so much joy and happiness because we put the wrong things first.

God, help me to appreciate all of the blessings you have put in my life. Amen.

NOT JUST ANOTHER NEW YEAR'S EVE

New year's Eve is always an exciting time to get out of the house and party and celebrate. For my wife and m,e howeMynstead just enjoyed having a quiet night taking the family out to a favorite restaurant, and then coming home and watching the festivities on television. This became our tradition, as dull and boring as it might have seemed for our children. We knew that in a few years, they would be finding their ways to ring in the new year with their friends, so we knew that this tradition would only be passed on to the two of us in the future.

I especially remember one New Year's Eve not because of the joy and excitement we shared but rather because of the awful turn of events that became very sobering for us. As we all sat at our table in the restaurant, we noticed several nearby people. They were having a very boisterous conversation about what the new year might bring. I couldn't help but overhear that they had many dreams and hopes of a future fulfilled with good fortune and dreams coming true.

As we were finishing our meal, the people at the other table were also finishing up and gathering their belongings to leave; what happened next could never have been anticipated by any of them or us.

As we were getting up to leave after they were gone, we were suddenly stunned by a loud sound of a collision. As the people who had sat next to us were pulling out of the parking lot, a speeding car coming the other way crashed into them. With such a violent and brutal collision taking place, we instantly knew that this accident was fatal for all of the passengers in both vehicles. I will never forget the twisted masses of steel and glass that shattered all over the highway. I couldn't speak I was so stunned and upset.

The following day we read in the newspaper that a drunk driver had caused the death of all 6 people. I was shocked that a new year would start offrant in such a fashion. I wondered many times what those victims had talked about as they looked forward to a new year. How different would their discussion have been if they had any idea that their lives here on earth were ready to end?

We know that our lives could end at any time. Do we just assume that tomorrow will come and we will focus on things that aren't important? Do we ever think about real life after death? Are we prepared to use the forgiveness of the sacrifice that God sent us in his son, Jesus, to bring us life everlasting in Heaven with God, or are we too busy planning our next days here on earth? Like that family on new year's eve, we can't be sure what tomorrow might bring.

QUESTION TO CONSIDER:

How often do you stop and think that your life could end at any time? Do we spend too much time on small things and not consider the big picture of our life?

REFEREEING A VOLLEYBALL GAME

Unless you've ever umpired or refereed a game, I don't think a person can understand how tense and difficult it can be. When I reffed high school volleyball, there would be some challenging times. Sometimes, as the ball went over the net, two or three players would jump up at the same time, the net would shake, the ball would come down, and some of the players would step over the line, all at the same time instant. The gym would suddenly get very quiet, and everyone would look at the official for the call. As the ref, you couldn't wait. You had to make your decision immediately, right or wrong, or both sides would start yelling and believe that you were just guessing.

One evening I had to travel to a small town about two hours away where two small schools had a fierce rivalry match. When I got there, I could feel the tension as I walked out onto the court and saw the small gym packed with excited fans. I think all the residents of both small towns were in that gym that night.

Everything seemed to be going quite well, even though I could sense that the fans who sat right behind me had already decided that I was the enemy and I was going to make calls that would favor the other team. Then it happened. Playing in such a small gym, it was inevitable that sometimes the ball would hit the ceiling. When it did, the ball came down on the same side, so the rule was that the team that hit the ball up to the roof could still play it. On this third hit, they hit the ball over the net to the other side and scored a point. The fans behind me began to yell that hitting the ball again after it hit the roof was not fair.

The match continued until the visiting team was ahead and ready to win a very close game. The home team returned what could have been the final point. The ball hit the roof, but the ball went over the net to the other team's side this time. I blew my whistle and gave the final and winning point to the visiting team. The home team crowd went wild and began screaming at me. They felt that since the last time I gave the point to the serving team but this time gave the point to the receiving team. They didn't realize that the rule was different when the ball passed over to the other side, and they didn't want to wait for an explanation.

I hurried off my ladder, grabbed my gym bag, and hurried out the side door. I never looked back. I jumped in my car and got on the road home as fast as I could.

Sometimes making the right decision and doing the right thing is not the easy thing to do. But we must stand up for what we believe is right and not be swayed by the most popular choice; We might have to act and not be able to explain why we did what we did. Being a non-consequentialist means that we must do the right thing regardless of the consequences.

QUESTION TO CONSIDER:

Do you ever back off from doing the right thing just because you are afraid of what other people might think?

THE CHAPEL LESSON

As a part of my job as principal of a Lutheran school, I would occasionally lead the weekly chapel service for all of the students. One of my favorite messages, which I probably used too often, was my surprise giving of a gift.

I would tell the students that today I would give someone five dollars. All they had to do was come up to the front of the church, and without having to do anything they would receive a five-dollar bill I had in my pocket.

At first, it would become hushed. Then, after a short time, one student would gather up the nerve to take a chance and come up front. As I handed that brave sole the money, the rest of the students would begin to regret that they didn't have the trust to come up and get the money.

I would then explain that since they didn't see the money, some of them weren't sure I had the five dollars to give them. Many people just can't believe something they can't see or prove. They lack the faith to trust God.

Others, were afraid to stand out in the crowd. They feared that others would judge and make fun of them for believing. How many people want to go along with the crowd and fit in with what the world expects of us?

Finally, some can't believe that we can get,t something without having to earn it. How can I get five dollars just by thinking someone will give me it without demanding anything? But this is precisely my point. God send His son to die for us so that we might be saved and be given eternal life. Why? What do we have to do to earn this gift? Accept it! Despite all our sins and failures, God's love for us gave us the most important gift ever. We can never measure up or earn this gift.

QUESTION TO CONSIDER:

Why is it so vital that we conform to what everyone else does and considers essential when we need to have the courage and strength to stand up and be willing to be different?

Lord, give me the courage to use your word to guide my life and not be afraid to stand out and walk in faith and love. Amen.

THE CHANGE IN HENRY

As the head soccer coach at a large high school, I had to deal with many young men and women who came from all walks of life and had different values and outlooks. Getting them to become one team and work together took time and patience and didn't always work, but after several weeks and some games, we started to play and act like a team. One student, in particular, a freshman named Henry, prticularlypecially challenging because he loved the attention and wanted to be the team clown. He loved to tease the other players and watch them get upset. He also loved to play pranks on them and watch them get embarrassed and upset. Fortunately, by the grace of God, we actually finished the season with a good record and with nobody wanting to kill someone.

Over the summer, something had happened to Henry. This cheerful, fun-loving free spirit had changed. He was now reticent and sad. He never smiled or laughed, and decided that, even though soccer had been his life's love, he would not play on the team again. He carried around a Bible everywhere he went, and never looked or spoke to anyone. He seemed like the saddest person I had ever known. When I approached him and asked him what changed him, he said that he had found God and now could no longer be part of a world that was so corrupt, sinful, and frivolous.

It made me so sad to see Henry this way. I don't believe that for one minute this is what God wants for us. He created such a beautiful and fantastic world for us, and He wants us to enjoy life and appreciate all of the blessings He gives to us. Even though we live in a world full of sin and sorry, I believe that by knowing that we have been saved, we can show our love for God by sharing joy and love with others.

I don't know what ever happened to Henry, but I pray that he eventually returned to the young man who lived a life of fun and happiness, maybe at least toned down some from his old nature.

QUESTION TO CONSIDER:

Do you ever miss out on many of the joys of living because of worry and guilt?

WHERE IS GOD?

God is a very loving God. But if this is true, why does He allow so many bad things to happen to us? We all experience some terrible times when we wish God would intervene and take away the pain and hurt. We have a hard time understanding why God would allow some things to come into our lives. Maybe this story of a summer adventure will help us understand more.

One sum,mer my wife and I decided that going on a white water rafting trip would be fun and exciting. We headed off to Tennessee and found the perfect rafting excursion-not too tricky for the five of us but challenging enough for us to make it an exciting adventure.

After signing a release and getting all of our necessary gear, we were given a short lesson on safety and rafting procedures. Now we were all ready to go. Into the raft, we climbed, and off we went.

As our guide navigated us along, we experienced some calm stretches and also some rockier parts of our trip. Then we suddenly went down some very swift rapids, and we all had to hang on tight to avoid falling out of the raft and tumbling into the rushing waters. At one point,nt my wife and our older daughter did fall out but could hang on to the raft wall and climb back in with the help of the guide. I now only noticed that we were not all alone on our voyage. Sitting on the banks of the river at several key locations were some of the employees of the adventure company. They let us experience some of the thrills and exciting waves without interfering. However, as it was explained to me later after we were back on shore, if, at any time, they felt that we were in real danger and might not be handle to handle things, they were prepared to jump in the waters and come to rescue. Someone was always there if the situation was more than we could handle.

In some ways, I think of God in this way. We have free will, and God lets us make decisions and choices. But He promises that He will not allow us to face more than we can handle. We can be assured that God is always with us and that he will never leave us. We can trust in Him, even when things happen that don't make sense to us, seem very unfair, and cause us so much pain and sorrow. Ultimately, through it all, our faith in Him and the sacrifice of His Son will bring us much greater joy and comfort than anything here on earth could.

QUESTION TO CONSIDER:

Why do we try to take control of our lives and turn to God only when we face trouble and sorrow? Can't we give our lives over to God every day and stay close to Him even when everything is going well?

Lord, take my life and use me for your purposes. Help me to trust that you will always be with me and direct me to what you desire for me. Amen.

SOMETIMES THE NUMBERS DON'T WORK

One night three businessmen checked into a hotel. Since it was late and the men were exhausted, they each chipped in $50 to pay for the room. The man who collected the money gave the $150 to the bellboy and told him to take the money to the front desk and use it to pay for the room.

When the bellboy gave the money to the clerk at the front desk, he was told that the room cost was only $130. He was given the change, $20, and told to return the extra money to the three men. On his way back to the room the bellboy decided that, since the numbers did not come out evenly, he would keep $5 for himself and give each of the three men $5 in change. He felt this was fair compensation for his time and trouble, and the men would never know the difference.

Now, let's analyze how the money came out. Since each of the three men paid $50 but got $5 back, they paid $45 each for the room. The bellboy kept $5. So the men paid $135, and the bellboy kept $5. That totals up to $140. But they started with $150. Where is the other $10?

Here it is again:

Three men each gave $50: $150

The actual cost of the room was $130. The change was $20.

From the change of $20, the bellboy kept $5. Each of the three men received $5 back: $15

So-we started with $150, the men paid $135, and the bellboy kept $5. WHERE IS THE OTHER $10?

If you go back and take $135 and then add $15 and $5, the numbers make sense. But why won't this work out when you figure it this way?

$45 x 3 + $5 equals $140?

When I have asked real mathematicians why this doesn't add up, I have never understood their explanations.

As a former math teacher, I learned to appreciate the consistency and exactness of working with numbers. Solving problems was very objective; either the answer was right or wrong. There was no questioning or debating the correctness of the answers.

Sometimes we want to look at situations and questions in our lives in the same way. We want clear and correct answers and struggle when things don't make sense to us. We want to understand and comprehend what and why things happen in our lives. If it can't be explained to our satisfaction, then we can't accept it. Something must be wrong.

This is the case that many people feel when we think of the existence of a superior being-God. We cannot understand so many elements of God. How could He always exist with no beginning or end? How could He be all-knowing and all-power? How could a loving God let many bad things happen to good people? So many other questions come to mind. It just doesn't make sense when we try to comprehend it all.

But here is the reality that we must understand. Our minds and our logic are so small and limited compared to God. We try to put things in our terms so we can comprehend them, but God's ways are far beyond our understanding. As one person once explained, trying to understand God's ways is like trying to explain the internet to an ant. We must trust God that He is in control and allows things to hapa pen that we just don't get.

What happens when we pray? Why does God sometimes grant us our wishes but at other times does not seem to hear us? Once again, we try to understand God and think we know better than God. When two teams play, both of them might pray for victory. Only one team can win. The winning team might walk away believing that God answered their prayer. What about the other team? Did they pray any less?

Once a young mother talked with a pastor about her son. The boy had been in a terrible accident and was now struggling for his life. The woman was bitter and told the pastor that if her innocent young son died, she would hate God and never pray again.

Years later, the pastor met the woman again. She told him her son did live, but his life went off course. He became addicted to drugs and was constantly in and out of prison. He brought much sorry and grief to his mother.

The mother admitted that she felt it would have been better for everyone if he had died after the accident. As a child, he knew Jesus as his Savior. The young man had rejected God and only brought misery and pain to everyone he met. She had been wrong.

God loves us and does know what is best for us, even if we don't understand why.

QUESTION TO CONSIDER:

Why do we believe we are smart enough to figure things out when there are so many mysteries of life that we can't explain? Why can't we accept the reality that God is in control of everything and we need to have enough faith to trust Him and believe that we can't understand and explain everything that happens to us?

Father, you love us and have plans for us. Let us turn our lives over to you and ask you to guide our lives. Amen.

DIFFERENT OUTCOMES

It was Sunday afternoon, and about a dozen young men played basketball in the school gym. The school had an open gym on Sundays, and the same guys showed up each week to get some exercise. A regular was John, the athletic director. John was several years older than the other players but was in good shape and could keep up with everyone.

The church pastor was working out in his yard when he received an urgent phone call. John was going up for a rebound when he suddenly crashed to the floor. He had passed out and was rushed to the hospital. His condition was severe.

When the pastor got to the emergency room, many people were waiting anxiously. John's wife saw the pastor enter the door and immediately rushed over to him to tell him what had happened. John had suffered a stroke, and only time would tell if he would recover or not.

Each day and night for the next week, the waiting room was filled with John's friends and family. The Pastor's church and many other surrounding churches held prayer vigils for John daily and night. The church, school members, John's family, and outside friends turned to God to save John's life that week. But John did not recover. Despite the constant attention of many doctors and nurses and all of the many prayers, John died the next Sunday. He was only 29 years old.

Several months after John's death, the daughter of one of the church members, Marie, also suffered a stroke. She was a senior at the local high school and was planning her valedictorian speech for her June graduation. Once again, members of the church, friends, and family spent many days and nights praying at the hospital and the local churches. For so many of them, it was hard to believe they were all going through this awful and heartbreaking situation again.

But this time, the patient survived. Even though she had lost much of her long-term memory, Marie came out of the coma and was able to go home soon afterward. She eventually returned to school and was able to continue with her educational plans, although not at the level she once was able to achieve. One of the doctors mentioned to the parents that her body reacted to low potassium levels, and if she had eaten a banana that morning, she might not have had the stroke. Nobody knew if that was true, but it was interesting to think about.

The obvious question in many people's minds after these two similar circumstances was why Marie lived, but John died. John was indeed prayed for as much. as Emily was. Both cases seemed so similar.

Of course, no one will ever know. Medical tests could not give anyone an answer. We can only accept that this was God's will and accept the reality that His will does not always make sense to us. How difficult this must be for the parents of John and his wife to take. We will not always understand, but we must always trust in God.

QUESTION TO CONSIDER:

Have you ever gotten angry at God because things didn't work out the way you wanted? Have you ever felt God has deserted you and no longer cares about you? Does God know better than you do what is best for you?

Lord, give us a solid faith to trust You completely and accept Your answers to our prayers. Amen.

OPENING THE LOCK

I don't believe that it should be difficult for many people to believe in God. They look around and see the beautiful sights of this world. The sky with clouds, beautiful sunsets, forests, canyons, oceans, and rivers are all evidence of a divine creator. Even the miracle of the birth of a newborn baby and the amazing way our bodies function prove that all of this just didn't happen by chance.

The only problem is that believing in a superior being that created our world is not enough. Unless one knows and accepts the sacrifice of Jesus for the forgiveness of sins, saying that they believe in God will not get someone to heaven. So if a person cannot discover God through his or her senses and experiences of nature, how can the true God be revealed?

Here is another chapel message that I liked to deliver to my students.

I would begin the message by holding up a combination lock and challenging everyone to figure out the combination that would open the lock. Now the older students knew better, but the younger boys and girls would all want a chance to open the lock and win a prize. Of course, the older students knew that there was no way that they could simply guess the combination, and the lock would open. With 40 numbers on the lock and three numbers on the combination, the probability of getting the correct numbers would be 40x39x39. That would be 60,840 possibilities.

After I let two or three children try to open the lock, I asked the audience what would they have to do to get the right combination. I could either tell them the numbers or they could read the correct combination that was printed on the tag that came with the lock.

The application is this. Unless a person reads the Bible or a devotional publication or is told the message of salvation, they cannot know the true God, the Triune God-Father, Son, and Holy Spirit. Our faith and belief in Jesus being sacrificed by a loving Father to redeem our sins can only be found through the work of the Holy Spirit.

The only way the Holy Spirit delivers this message of salvation is for someone to read about God or be told. This is where we come in. This is God's plan. We must tell others about the Triune God and the Bible. Without the help of others, a person cannot figure out that God the Father sent His Son Jesus to earth the save us from our sins. The Holy Spirit opens our hearts to God and enables us to believe. It is only through the True God that a person can be saved.

QUESTION TO CONSIDER:

Does it bother you when others criticize you for being narrow-minded about religion? Why do they feel that we are we so arrogant that we insist our beliefs are true?

Heavenly Father, when we center our beliefs around your word, the Bible, we know the truth—that You created us, and then saved us through the sacrifice of your Son, Jesus Christ. Without Jesus, there is no salvation. Amen.

FORGIVING OTHERS

Once there was an excellent basketball player who was a star in both college and the pros. After his playing days were over he went on to coach and led his team to two consecutive NBA world championships. But it was one night in 1977 that changed his life forever.

Rudy was playing that night in a very physical professional basketball game against the Lakers when a fight broke out between several players on the two teams. Rudy ran over to break up a fight when one of the players on the Lakers punched him in the face. Rudy was nearly killed and was rushed to the nearby hospital. Although, after several surgeries, Rudy recovered, his career was never the same. Rudy Tomjanovich describes this awful night in the book, The Punch, written by John Feinstein.

When writers interviewed him in the hospital, he was asked if the other player had ever contacted him to say he was sorry for the brutal blow. Rudy admitted that his assailant had made no effort to get him.

When asked if he now carried a deep hatred for Kermit, Rudy responded, "It took me a long time to get to the point where I could think about him without feeling resentment. Right from the beginning, I knew that to recover, I couldn't afford to hate him, that if I did, it would be like taking poison and hoping that someone else would die from it." (p 342)

If there is someone in your life who you have a strong dislike for, even hatred, we can learn from Rudy. Give it up. First, God tells us that we must forgive others if we are to be ignored. Secondly, carrying around this "poison" in us doesn't hurt the other person. They probably don't even know how much we hate them, or maybe they're glad we are making ourselves miserable. Hatred hurts only us. We carry around all of this bitterness and horror, which only brings us down.

Now I know that forgiving is not always an easy thing to do. Maybe someone has done something to our loved ones that were awful or us.

I remember a teacher I had on my staff who would get depressed at the same time every year. She needed to take a day or two off because of how this feeling would affect her. When I asked what the problem was, she told me that it was at this time of the year that a drunk driver had killed her parents. How is someone going to ever forgive the drunken driver for that?

Well, we can't-- at least not by ourselves. But God can work in our hearts and with his help, we can move on and not let hatred control us. Think of the survivors of the Holocaust or the parents that lost children in one of the school shootings. We must give up our hatred by turning to God and asking Him to give us the strength we need. We must turn the guilty over to Him and let Him deal with it. As God said, "Vengeance is mine." Leave the justice we seek in life over to Him.

QUESTION TO CONSIDER:

Is there anyone for who you have very strongtowardelings of dislike or hatred? What purpose does this have? Aren't you punishing only yourself?

God, sometimes there are times when we feel that we can't find the mercy to forgive someone. Give us the grace to forgive. Amen.

DO YOU CARE?

When I moved to Houston, one of my priorities was locating a health club close to my new home. As I drove around the neighborhood I found a club just a few blocks from home. I went inside to check the place out. As I approached the front desk, I was greeted by a young lady who asked me if she could help. When I told her I wanted some information and a club tour, she said she would be glad to help and paged a sales representative.

As I waited, I glanced around the workout area, and everything seemed pretty typical of an average workout gym. There was a wide variety of fitness seekers, from new beginners to muscle-bound experienced lifters. The fitness machines and weights were similar to the apparatus that I was used to using.

Just then, the fitness advisor approached and stuck out his hand. He was pretty young, obviously in good shape, and looked very efficient with his clipboard, official club shirt, and name tag.

He introduced himself as Mark and asked what my name was. From the start, I understood that Mark didn't care about my name or anything else. He seemed more interested in a pretty young girl working in a tight outfit in the far corner. When I told him my name and began explaining my fitness goals, he kept looking down at his clipboard. Then he raised his head and started looking around to see who was working out. I doubted if he even heard my name, and he certainly didn't listen at all when I described what my fitness needs were. Even before I could finish telling him about myself, he interrupted me and suggested that we walk around the club so that he could show me the facilities.

The conversation during the brief tour was one-sided and centered only on his workouts. He told me where he was from and his hopes for his future in the fitness business. He never asked me any questions and seemed more interested in greeting the members of the club as they passed by, especially the attractive female ones. When we finished the tour, we went into his "office," a desk and two chairs in a small cubicle among several other little workspaces. He got down to the various membership options, begin- ning with the most expensive one. Then he handed me some papers that gave the club's operation hours and rules.

He asked me if I was ready to join and wanted me to sign-up and set up payments on my credit card. As soon as I told him that I wanted to take home the papers and read them and then think about it, he abruptly got up, mumbled "fine," and returned to the front counter to introduce himself to another prospective member.

I'll never forget how this experience made me feel. We all have had times when we were made to feel unimportant. Incidents such as these serve as a stark reminder that we too often think only,y of ourselves and don't care about anyone else, especially those we don't know or don't want to know. Our little universe often revolves around only our wants and needs, and there is little room for anyone or anything else. We wake up each morning planning how we and others can satisfy our wants and desires. What will make us happy and bring us satisfaction and attention?

Most of us have jobs that involve working with others. Pleasing them and satisfying their needs are usually part of our necessary goals. But ask yourself-do if you genuinely care about them. Do you get to know them and try to understand what their life is like? It seems hard to not always to put ourselves first and only want whatever is best for us.

Once I saw a car that had an interesting bumper sticker. The sticker's message was straightforward, "It's all about me!" Even though our initial response to such a message might be how could anyone want to be labeled this way, at least we can give the driver credit for being honest. Why be a hypocrite or pretend that we want to live our lives in service to others if we are living only for our pleasure and satisfaction?

One time a man walked into a car dealer's showroom and asked to be shown the most expensive model the dealer sold. The re-receptionist, sensing the importance of a possible sale, called for the most knowledgeable salesman working that day. When this top-selling salesman came to the front desk, he immediately attempted to impress the potential customer with how much knowledge he had about the car. He spent many hours with the man explaining all of the numerous features and advantages that this expensive car had to offer. At the end of the lengthy demonstration, the customer decided he would not purchase the vehicle. As he was walking out the door, the owner of the dealership rushed over and asked the man if he could talk with him for just another few minutes. The man agreed, and they went into the owner's office. Fifteen minutes later, the man who had initially decided not to buy the car had changed his mind and signed the contract. One of the other salespeople, who had witnessed this whole scenario, was puzzled at the turn of events. Later that morning he had a chance to ask the owner how he had succeeded in selling the car after the top salesman on the floor had failed. The owner answered him this way.

"I know that Jim knows more about these cars than anyone else here, including me. He knows cars, but he never did get to see the customer. After taking a few minutes to understand the buyer, I showed him that I cared about him and explained why this car would satisfy his needs. The customer could sense the difference. He could tell that I just didn't want to make a sale, but I wanted him to get the car that he liked. When he felt I wanted him to be happy, he trusted me and went ahead with the purchase."

This story reminds me of the old saying: nobody cares how much you know until they know how much you care. If we genuinely care about people and want to serve them rather than just get them to buy into our plan, we will be much more successful in the long run. The same is true in dealing with others in our lives. If we can put the needs and wants of others first and sincerely serve them, we know that it is pleasing to God to live our lives this way. People will recognize and appreciate this attitude and want to be with us. Just as I couldn't get past the fitness club representative's at- attitude to even consider joining, when others sense that we are being selfish and thinking only of ourselves, they will not trust us or even listen to what we say.

Caring about others is not only how God wants us to live our lives; it's also the most effective way to do business. I remember hearing it put this way. We need to be third. First is God. Secondly should come others. Then we put ourselves third. I realize this is very difficult because with our original sin comes a need to be selfish and think only of ourselves. Just as we find that giving is more blessed than receiving, we can find so much more satisfaction in our lives when we sacrifice and love others. God will bless us.

QUESTION TO CONSIDER:

Do you listen to what others have to say, or are you busy thinking about what you want to say? Do we care what they say?

Lord, give us the heart to genuinely care for others and not just center our lives on ourselves. Amen.

TAKE ME TO THE CROSS

There was once a young boy who got lost in the big city. He was terrified and felt alone as he wandered through the streets, searching for anything or anyone who might help him find his way back home. Finally, after many long hours of frustration and failure, he gave up. He sat on the curb and began to cry. He just didn't know where to turn or what to do now.

Just then, a police car pulled up to him, and the window rolled down. The policeman asked him what was wrong.

"I've lost my way, and don't know how to get back home." The little boy sobbed.

"Jump in," the big policeman told the boy. "We will drive around until we find something to help you remember where you live."

The little boy quickly got into the car and felt a warm feeling of re- lief. Surely he would be able to get back to where he wanted to be so bad. But as the police car drove down the street after street, they all looked the same and the little boy still didn't see anything that looked familiar. A feeling of fear began to return as he wondered if he would ever get back to where he was loved and felt safe.

"Don't get discouraged, son." The officer said. "Sooner or later you will see something that will help you find your way back home. Can you think of any landmarks such as a store or building to help us know which neighborhood you are looking for?"

The little boy thought for a while and then suddenly blurted out, "Yes, there is a big church on the corner of my street with a large cross in front. Take me to the cross, and I can find a way back!"

"Great, I know where that cross is, and we can take you there," assured the policeman. "Then you can figure out how to get home."

Once the boy saw the cross, he knew where his home was, and he rushed out of the car and into the front door of his house, where his mother and father were there to hold him in their arms and comfort him in the safety of a loving and caring environment.

Why is it vital that we raise our children in the church and teach them about their loving Father in Heaven, who will never leave or desert them? Just as the young boy lost his way in the big city, it is easy for young people to lose their way on their own for the first time. There are so many dead ends, and wrong turns that anyone can follow that will take them away from the life God wants.

A member of our church board once questioned the value of Christian education. He was aware of how much money operating a school costs the church and was upset with the behavior of several of our high school graduates when they moved on to adulthood. He felt their attitude and behavior did not properly represent our school or church.

He didn't realize that when some young men and women go out on their own and suddenly have the freedom to make their own choices, they are tempted to follow a path of rebellion and experimentation that can lead to unwanted consequences. But when we give a child a firm foundation in faith early in life, they can find their way back to the cross. They will be able to use what they have been taught to see God again. This foundation is that cross that will guide them back. The seed of faith planted by the Holy Spirit in them as young people will now be able to grow once again. Without this foundation, this landmark, this cross, they will have nothing to turn to when difficult times and temptations come into their lives. We must equip them to weather the storms of life and turn to the loving arms of a merciful savior.

QUESTION TO CONSIDER:

Are there times in your life when you feel distant from God? What brings you back to Him?

Lord, when we feel apart from You help us to be reassured that You will never leave us—it is us pulling away from You. You will always be there for us. Amen.

AT A FOOTBALL GAME - URGENCY

Have you ever attended a major sporting event? Here in Texas, the football rules. Over 100,000 football fans fill a stadium to cheer on the beloved home team on five or six Saturdays each Fall. Sitting in the upper section of the vast stadium, it is pretty impressive to see so many people of all types gathered in one place. You can relate if you live in a city with a large university.

Did it ever occur to you that every one of those spectators, who have such a passion for a sporting event, will all someday die? Nobody knows where or when this will happen, but it certainly will.

How many of them have heard the message of salvation? Do they all realize that they are sinful, and without the forgiveness of sins earned for them through the death and resurrection of a Savior, they will not be in Heaven for all eternity? Do we not feel any urgency in bringing the Word to others?

I realize we flash a message on the massive Jumbotron during halftime that will open 100,000 hearts to the Holy Spirit. During an exciting college football game is probably not the time or place to interrupt the action on the field. That is not what I am saying we need to do. There is a time and place for everything. But my point is this- how can we comfortably sit back and accept the reality that everyone needs Jesus, who died for all? What are we doing? Shouldn't we at least be uncomfortable with the fact that there are so many people who, for some reason or another, don't even have a clue that their fate for all of eternity is hanging on the balance of accepting the gift of salvation that has been given to them by a merciful God? How can we open up their hearts and souls to the Holy Spirit to believe?

Enjoy the game. But can't we pray and commit to changing our community sometime somewhere? God has given us this task. What are we going to do about it?

QUESTION TO CONSIDER:

Do you ever feel guilty when you hear about people who do not ac- accept Jesus as their savior? What can we do about it?

God, help us to spread Your message. Amen.

HELPING JOHN

The father was down to his last hope. His wife had just died, and now his young son, John, needed help. The young boy had a list of quite a few disabilities and had not been able to make it to several public schools. Now, with the death of his mother, his father knew that John was about to give up. John had been very close to his mother. Not knowing where to turn, Dad hoped that a private, Christian school might be his son's only chance. After being turned away at several Christian schools, he called me. I told him I would be glad to meet with him and his son that afternoon.

As I greeted John and his father that day, I saw two individuals who had been beaten down with the pain and sorrow of losing the center of their very existence.

Mr. Williams was very nervous and anxious as he sat in my office. John just seemed very distant as he stared at the ceiling.

As I asked several questions, my heart ached for them. I wanted to help and knew that the decision was up to me. As principal, the fate of these two hurting souls was in my hands. I did have a copy of John's records from his previous schools and felt that it would take an act of God for him to be able to be successful in our fourth-grade class. After talking more with them, I finally decided to give John a chance. But before I could tell Mr. Williams the excellent news, I felt that I had to at least talk with the fifth-grade teacher. The fifth-grade teacher happened to be my wife.

At first, Peggy was not sure we would be doing the right thing. Would letting John in our school be the best thing for all of the other students and John? But as we continued to talk and I reminded her that he had just lost his mother, she agreed that we could at least try.

When I called Mr. Williams later that day, he seemed relieved and excited. I reminded him that this would only be a trial and that if my wife and I felt things were not working out, we would have to ask John to leave. Under those terms, the father did agree to the plan.

At first, John started out doing reasonably well. He was quite a bit behind the rest of the class, but at least he was behaving and didn't seem to be too frustrated or discouraged. Peggy also believed that he was learning and that this did seem to be working out. But after several weeks, it became apparent that this was not the best place for John. Both Peggy and I wanted John to be successful, but we finally had to face the truth. John's emotional changes were impossible, and he could not adjust to the other students' classroom routines. In addition to this, he was way behind, and catching up under these circumstances did not seem possible anymore. On Friday, after John had spent four weeks in the class, I had to call up Mr. Williams and tell him that John could not stay in the school any longer. He would have to make other arrangements for next week.

When the father and son came into my office after school that day, Mr. Williams was heartbroken. I looked at poor John and told the father, "I'm so sorry. I wanted so much for this to work. I feel that I have let you and John down. I'm sorry, but we tried and just could not win this one. It is not the best thing for the teacher, the class, and especally John."

The father looked down for a very long time, and I could see the tears in his eyes. He finally put his arm around John and looked up at me.

Please don't feel that you failed. John and I appreciate all the time and care you and your wife showed to my son. He felt loved here, and you both helped him start to get over losing his mother."

I was glad and relieved that the father had understood and accepted my decision so well, but I never expected to hear what he said next.

"You know, when I brought John here we were both lost after my wife's death. I was ready to give up on John and myself. But then John came home each day and we talked about what went on, especially what he learned in religion class. I had never been a churchgoer, but after listening to my son every day, I decided that I would honor his request and take him to church. We even began to read a holy book and the Bible together. We kept going to church every Sunday, and now I have become an Elder in the church. Our new relationship with God has turned our lives around, and we can now find the strength to go on and face the world together."

As I shook his hand and hugged John, I thought about how God works in ways we never planned. Peggy and I had thought we had failed and nothing good could come of this wrong decision. But now we understood that God had another plan and a way to make this a victory. Things didn't work out for John the way we had hoped, but along the way, he and his father found their way out of the darkness and into the light of God.

How often do we not look beyond the immediate moment and see another side of things? We never really know what a difference we can make in others' lives in the long run. God can use us in a way that we might never understand. Just a kind word, a smile, or a loving action can change someone's life in a way we never realize. Each day we have to ask ourselves how we can be a blessing to someone today. God will make it happen and use us to make that difference.

QUESTION TO CONSIDER:

Did you ever feel discouraged because you believed that you failed in your attempt to help others? Is it possible that you didn't see the good that you did?

Lord, may we trust in you that our good deeds might help others even if we don't see the results. Amen.

THE BOY IN THE DINER

Bonnie had been waiting on tables in the small diner for six years now, and she was getting tired of it. Being on her feet all day, acting friendly to people who just took her for granted and only wanted her to wait on their every need and bring their food to them quickly was finally getting to her. She knew her attitude was turning sour, and she was ready to tell off the next customer, throw their food at them, and walk out forever. It was just one of those moments and just one of those days.

But, of course, she needed the money and she needed to keep the job. The hourly pay was pathetic, but the tips enabled her to survive from week to week. That's why she judged and treated customers based on how much of a tip she thought they would leave. Why work hard and be friendly to someone if she knew they would not leave her with a decent tip?

Just then, as she was thinking about her plight and feeling sorry for herself, in walked a young boy. It was slow that day, so he just went to an open table and sat down. Bonnie waited a while and finally forced herself to get up and walk over to him. She knew she would be lucky if he even left her a tip.

"What do you want?" she snarled at him.

The young boy put down the gravy-stained menu and ordered a hamburger, fries, and water. "Big deal," she thought. "With this order of three fifty, I might get a quarter tip if I'm lucky."

She brought the boy his food and then went and sat down in another section. Soon she saw the boy wave to her. "Great! Now for his 25-cent tip, I have to return and give him more service," she grumbled.

"What will it be now?" she snapped at him. "How much does a piece of pie cost?"

"I guess he couldn't even read the menu and figure that out for himself," she thought.

"One dollar and twenty-five cents. Shall I bring you a piece?"

The boy paused and responded, "No thanks, I only have five dollars, so I can't afford the dessert."

"Don't they teach math in school anymore?" the waitress thought.

"Son, you do have enough money. Even with the pie, you will still be under five dollars."

"Oh no," he answered. "If I did that, I wouldn't have enough money to give you a decent tip. I'll just have to go without the pie."

She took the five-dollar bill off the table as he walked out the door, cashed out his check, and then kept her tip. Maybe she should have been nicer to him after all.

How often do we judge someone to discover that we were wrong about them? Some people go through their lives thinking the worst of people. They believe that the person driving so slowly in front of them is doing it just to bother them or when they take too much time pulling out of a parking space they want.

Their being so slow is making us mad. The world is against us, and everyone is out to get us.

What a miserable way to live. Instead, we will be much happier when we put the best construction on things. Besides, even if someone hurts our feelings with a rude or insensitive remark, can't we accept the fact that we all are human and say and do things that are not right? Are we perfect? Then why do we expect others to be?

QUESTION TO CONSIDER:

Did you ever think poorly of someone and then change your outlook after you got to know them?

God, give us the patience and understanding to put the best construction on what others say and do. Amen.

A DAUGHTER'S WISDOM-THE SNAKE

My daughter, Joy, has always had a big heart, especially for those who need help. In high school, she became involved with a young man who certainly did need someone to help him. He had spent some time in jail and was now attending the same high school with her. She believed she could help and positively influence him, but my wife and I were concerned about this relationship.

After many days of worry and fear, I decided that Joy and I needed to have a long talk about Abe. I wanted to explain, in a very sensitive and friendly way, why she was wasting her time trying to change him and how she was only bringing herself down. As it turned out, the story kind of backfired, and I was the one who learned a lesson. Here's the story that I thought would teach her a lesson.

Once there was a man who was crossing through the woods. As he reached about halfway, he thought he heard a voice. He looked down, and there was a snake at his feet. He pulled away instantly because he could quickly tell the snake was poisonous.

"Oh, please don't be afraid of me." whispered the snake. "I have a big favor to ask of you. I am very tired of crawling through this dense underbrush. Would you please do me a big favor and pick me up and carry me for a while?"

"Are you kidding?" replied the surprised hiker. "You are a very deadly snake. If I picked you up, you would bite me, and I would die. I just want to get away from you as quickly as I can. Goodbye."

"Oh please, kind sir, take pity on me. It is so hot, and I am so tired. I can't help it that I was born this way. I want to change and start a new future. I would be forever grateful. Besides, if you would do this big favor for me, do you think I would show my appreciation by hurting you? I would never bite you after you showed me such kindness."

The man thought it over for a minute and then replied, "Well, I guess I could help you and carry you for a little while. It's not your fault that God made you this way. I didn't think you would bite me if I came to your aid. After all, the Bible tells us that we should love others and show kindness and mercy to everyone. Come over here, and I will help you up."

As soon as the man picked up the snake, the snake turned on him and bit him. Crying out in pain the startled man fell to the ground.

"Why did you do that?" the man screamed. "You promised me that you would not repay my kindness this way. I trusted you, and this is the thanks I get. You took advantage of me and betrayed me!"

The snake looked down on the man and laughed.

"Why are you blaming me for this? You knew what I was right from the start. Snakes bite people--this is who we are. Why are you surprised? You knew better."

As I looked at the reaction on my daughter's face, I hoped that this story would help her see that, although she meant well, she had to accept the reality that this young man just wasn't going to change. She was only going to get hurt.

"Joy, do you see that your friend is like this snake? You know who he is. Just like the snake, you will not be able to change him. Nothing can change someone like that. Joy looked at me and replied, " Dad, the Holy Spirit can help me change him."

How could I reply to that? One time, a father was the student, and my daughter was the teacher.

Is there a time when we must say no to helping someone? A friend of mine put it this way. "God wants us to be soft-hearted, not soft-headed."

As we try to deal with others who seem full of hatred and revenge and are angry and spiteful, we must be careful. Sometimes we must walk away and pray for them because they seem to reject us and anything we are trying to do.

As it turned out, our daughter finally realized that nothing she tried was working. Unfortunately for the young man, life only got worse. Maybe the fact that she wanted to help him had made her feel better about things.

QUESTION TO CONSIDER:

Have you changed your life and become a better person as you grow older?

God, just as the Holy Spirit changed Saul to Paul, you have the power to soften the hearts of people and turn their lives around. Amen.

A SUPER BOWL TO REMEMBER

Tomorrow would be another "Super Sunday" when the San Francisco 49ers and the Ravens would face off in Super Bowl XLVI. Whenever I think of past Super Bowls, I remember some more than others. As it turned out, this one meant the most to me, even though I didn't even get to see it.

Earlier that week, my Pastor came up to me and asked me if I would be willing to do a big favor for one of the members of his church. He explained that a significantly older man had been contacted by his brother, who told him he needed to come and visit him as soon as possible. His brother said this might be the last time such a visit would be possible. The doctor had told his brother that he was slipping fast and might not last for another week or two.

The church member went to the pastor and asked him if there might be someone in the congregation who would be able to drive him to see his brother as soon as possible. The trip down to Sarasota was only a couple of hours away, but it would have to be as quick as his brother could have a visitor, which happened to be on the following Sunday. As it turned out, the next Sunday was the day of the Super Bowl. Talk about some guilt.

"Why me?" I kept wondering. I kept thinking that there must be many others, especially older women, who wouldn't mind missing the game at all. But the pastor had asked me what I could say. Would I tell him I couldn't help someone in real trouble because I wanted to watch a football game?

Fortunately, my wife helped me realize what I really should do, so I said yes.

The elderly gentleman and I got an early start the following day. When we arrived at the hospital we got help locating the room where the brother was. I left for a while so the two brothers would have plenty of time. Finally, it came time for the patient to get some rest, and the passenger entered the waiting room and was ready to return home. As I looked at him, I could look beyond the tears in his eyes and sensed that he was now at peace with the inevitable outcome. This precious time he could spend with his brother would help him get through the tough times ahead.

On the way home I did get to listen to some of the game on the radio. Although I don't remember the outcome, I must admit that I will never forget that "Super Sunday."

I don't tell this story to give myself credit or praise. I'm sure that without my wife's encouragement and the guilt I felt, I might have said no and stayed home and watched the game. Sometimes our motivation for helping others is just a reaction to responsibility and concern about what others might think of us. But thankfully, sometimes God inspires us to make decisions in our lives to do the right thing when we are tempted to turn away and selfishly think only of ourselves. And a good wife certainly doesn't hurt, either.

QUESTION TO CONSIDER:

Have you ever told someone no when they asked for help because you didn't want to give up the time or comfort to come to their aid? Did you feel guilty afterward?

Lord, help us to be there for others and think not just of ourselves and what we want. Amen.

GUILT - THE LITTLE GIRL AND HER DAD

One of the most significant obstacles we must continually overcome in our lives is guilt. Too often, we find ourselves haunted by things in the past that we didn't handle well. We can't forget and shake away memories and consequences of mistakes we made in our lives, so we languish in self-pity and keep replaying the past in our minds. If you think you have a moment in your history that is hard to get over, let me tell you about Phil.

Phil and I were classmates in college and played on the baseball team. He batted second, and I batted third. I remember one game when Phil failed to drive in the tying run on second. He got so angry that he threw his bat in the corner of the dugout, put his head down, and pouted. When I came up and drove in the tying run, he was the first to congratulate me.

After we graduated, Phil moved to New Jersey, and I moved to Florida. At first, we kept in touch, but the letters became fewer and fewer after a while. In his last letter, Phil told me that he had gotten a good job, married, and had a daughter he adored. I was glad that everything had worked out so well for Phil.

Several years later I met another former classmate and he asked me if I had heard the latest news about Phil. First of all, Phil had gotten into drugs and alcohol. His marriage was falling apart, and his job was heading toward failure. He was now in debt and would soon lose his house, marriage, and career. And then, as if Phil didn't have enough problems, that one morning on that one summer day happened.

Every morning before going to work Phil would get all ready for work and then spend a few minutes on his front porch, just relaxing with a cup of coffee. One morning, as he was just prepared to sit down and enjoy his hot drink, his young daughter suddenly pushed open the screen door and went to sit on his lap. She was just so excited to come to her dad! Unfortunately, when she jumped up on him, she knocked his cup of hot coffee all over his white dress shirt. His natural reaction was to scream out when he felt that hot coffee spill all over him.

His yell scared his little girl. She jumped out of his lap and ran away, heading down the sidewalk and into the busy street. Just then, a passing truck tried to swerve but couldn't avoid hitting her. Her little body, still in her pajamas, flew into the gutter. Phil ran out to her and bent down over her.

"I'm sorry, Daddy," she whispered as he looked down into her tear-filled blue eyes. At that moment, he knew that those words would be her last. Her little body went limp, and Phil hugged her so tightly. The unimaginable had happened. He lost the one thing in life that meant the most to him. He lost his innocent and precious little angel.

After telling me this story, my friend, with tears in his eyes, said to me that after this had happened, Phil was never the same. He lost his job, and his wife left him. His whole life had fallen apart, and now he was alone, in debt, and haunted every minute by that one quick moment in his life.

I couldn't believe something like this could have happened to Phil or anyone. How could anyone go on with his life having to bear such guilt and sorrow? All I could do was close my eyes every morning and night and pray for Phil.

For the next few days, I couldn't get Phil off of my mind. I tried to call him but his number was no longer in service. I couldn't even write to him because I had lost his address long ago. Even other friends who had written to Phil did not get any response.

The years passed, and gradually, I forgot about Phil. Then, one morning, I received a letter from the friend who had first told me about Phil. I couldn't believe the update.

Phil had pulled his life together. He stopped his drug and alcohol abuse. He and his wife reconnected through all the suffering. He found a new job and was once again secure. He had become successful and had been promoted several times. He and his wife had another little girl, who was now three. And best of all, he had found Christ and used his faith to help his recovery. I felt great relief and joy as I read the good news.

Of course, the awful morning accident was not a blessing or a good thing. No one would ever wish anything like that to happen to anyone. But it did serve as a wake-up call to Phil, and he did turn his life around after the incident. He and his wife suddenly realized how much they needed the support of each other to survive. And they were able to turn to God for strength. In his darkest hour, Phil refused to give up.

The lesson we can learn from this shocking story is this. No matter how unworthy we feel to receive God's love, blessing, and forgiveness, He will still be there for us. He will never desert us, and no matter how down we get about ourselves and our mistakes and sins in life, we can still turn to Him in our self-pity and sorrow and say, "God, here I am. Please forgive me and let me turn my miserable and pathetic life over to you. Even though I can't understand why you still love me, your unconditional love will never fail me."

Just think, if Phil can overcome his shame and guilt, then you can be sure that you can overcome your past and face a new day washed in the blood of our Savior; you are clean and fresh again.

QUESTION TO CONSIDER:

Is there anything from your past that you can't seem to get over and move on from it? Is it keeping you from finding peace in the present and future?

God, when we turn to You for forgiveness, Thank you for the assurance that You will not only forgive us but also forget what we did. Amen.

THE RAILROAD CROSSING

As principal of a school, my job was to lead the various programs offered. In addition to our regular classes and after-school activities, we also provided an after-school service for students who couldn't be picked up until their parents left work at five o'clock or later. Many of these students also attended our regular school, but some were picked up from other nearby schools to wait for their parents. One day I wanted to meet these other boys and girls who were not students of our school but did come there to be picked up.

As I greeted these children I had never met, I couldn't help but notice one little girl in particular. She was probably in third or fourth grade and was very pretty. But as I returned her smile, I saw a certain glow that seemed to be coming from her. There was something about her that set her apart from all of the others. I had never seen anything like it.

As I walked back to my office, I couldn't get over what I had just ex- experienced. I felt an aura of some kind when I saw her.

Later that day, as I was getting ready to go home, I suddenly got an urgent message on the phone. One of our students had been involved in a tragic accident. I was told to turn on the television immediately. I turned on the news, and a reporter was near our school telling the story. He reported that a parent was driving his daughter home, and he, for some reason, tried to get through a railroad crossing as an oncoming train approached. Even though the lights flashed, he beat the lowering gates and went into the intersection. The train hit the car.

The reporter said that, although the driver was uninjured, the train had crashed into the back of his car, and his daughter, who was alone in the backseat, had been fatally injured by the crash. Then a picture of the girl killed was flashed on the screen; it was the young girl I had met that afternoon.

Several days later, at the funeral, the driver, the girl's mother's boyfriend, told everyone how much he had loved the little girl and wondered how he and the girl's mother would recover from this. But in addition to his overwhelming guilt, he now faced possible criminal charges for running the train crossing lights.

Once again, as in Phil's story, I saw someone who had a tremendous mistake to try and overcome. What could he say to the little girl's mother to improve things? It was just one foolish mistake, but the consequences would last for the rest of his life.

But, as I reflect on this terrible occurrence, I can't help but think about the girl. Why did I just happen to visit the aftercare that particular day? Why did that little girl stand out to me, and why did I see a glow around her? Is it possible that this accident was God's plan for her that day? Was this not just a senseless lack of good judgment on the driver's part or God's plan for that day? Maybe when we feel guilty about something, we are carrying out an action that God is directing.

QUESTION TO CONSIDER:

Did you ever do something stupid and can't figure out why you did it? Were you able to move on?

God, we ask that you give us the gift of forgiveness for others and ourselves. Amen.

OUR DOG PEANUT

When my son moved into an apartment, he couldn't bring his two dogs with him, so I brought them to my house. At the time, we both knew that it would be hard for my family and me to give them back. It didn't take them long to become a part of our family.

They were both little dogs and were mixed breeds, and I didn't know what their mixture was. They each had their personalities. Peanut, short for peanut butter, was very shy and very mild-tempered. I don't think any of us ever heard him growl or bark. Shorty was a bit more outgoing, but she, too, was reticent. It didn't take her as long to feel comfortable and fit into our household. Although it took Peanut more time to get to know us, he became our "baby." He was very affectionate and loved to sit on our laps and be petted. These two little dogs brought us so much joy and love.

One day my wife came home from school and didn't see Peanut. After searching around the house, she opened the back door to see if he was in the backyard. She immediately saw Peanut lying down near the porch. When she came closer to him she saw that he wasn't just asleep, he was passed out. She quickly picked him up, brought him into the house, and held him in her arms until I came home about an hour later.

When I walked into the room, I could tell that Peanut was not ok. I said to my wife that he didn't seem to be breathing, so I told her that we must take him to the veterinarian's office immediately.

The animal hospital was not very far away. I carried Peanut in and gave him to the vet's assistant, and she brought him into one of the rooms so that the vet could quickly examine him. As we waited outside in the reception room, we worried but couldn't believe that Peanut would not wake up and everything would be fine.

A few minutes later, the vet told us Peanut would not be waking up. She said she could keep trying but felt it would not make a difference. Peanut had died of heart failure. She would not be coming home with us after all.

Of course, my wife and I and our daughter and granddaughter cried all night. Peanut was such a sweet and innocent little dog who never was mean or would hurt anything. He was just so loving and meant so much to us.

As the four of us talked later, we tried to explain how this could have happened. We wanted to find some explanation to vent our hurt and anger, and we sure did. First, our daughter thought Peanut was in the house when she left for work that afternoon. Shorty came in, but she forgot about Peanut. It was boiling that day, so the poor dog was left in the hot sun for several hours. It was her fault.

But when my wife came home, why didn't she see that Peanut was not well, and why didn't she take him quickly to the vet? From the time she got home until we finally did take him probably made a difference. She was to blame.

But then she raised an interesting question. A few days before, she had asked me to take Peanut and get his fur trimmed. I told her we could wait another week and save some money. Perhaps if he had been cut, the heatbeen couldn't have affected him so m much, so maybe I was to blame.

Do you ever find yourself searching for someone or something to blame when something goes wrong? Do we want to find guilt in others because we don't want to feel guilty about what has happened? Here again, responsibility plays a big part in keeping us under the dark cloud of sin.

Maybe Peanut had a weak heart, and none of these "mistakes" we each made caused his death. Some things in life just happen. We might search for explanations for our past sins and mistakes, but thankfully we have a loving God who doesn't dwell on our past. Unlike other people, God can not only forgive our shortcomings, but He also can forget them. In the Bible, we are told this about our forgiving God:

"For as high as the heavens are above the earth, so great is His love for those who fear Him; as far as the east is from the west, so far has He removed our transgressions from us." (Psalm 103, verses 11 and 12)

The story's point is this: blaming one another or ourselves doesn't help. It won't bring Peanut back. Instead, we must recognize and admit that we are all human and often make mistakes and sin. Forgiving others and ourselves is more important than keeping score of our errors and bad judgments. Loving and comforting each other through hard times is much better than pointing fingers and finding fault and blame. God still loves us despite our weaknesses and flaws.

QUESTION TO CONSIDER:

Have you ever spent so much time and energy trying to find blame that you didn't have the opportunity to fix the problem?

God, we admit that we sin daily and need Your forgiveness. We know we are guilty sinners. Amen.

PLAYOFF SEATS

Being the principal of a school is not always an easy job, but it can have its perks. Gifts from parents are lovely to receive--especially tickets to sporting events. One day a father of two boys in our school called me and asked if I would like to join them that afternoon to watch the first game of a playoff series between the Houston Astros and the San Diego Padres. The company he worked for had given him the tickets, and he had an extra one. Of course, I never hesitated. Not only was this going to be a great game, but I had always liked the man and his sons.

As soon as school,l ended, the father was in the parking lot waiting for us. Thirty minutes later we were at the ticket gate at the Astrodome. Much to my surprise, these were not just ordinary seats. We took the elevator up to the corporate boxes on the second level. When we entered the small room, several rows of chairs faced the field, surrounded by televisions and food. There were nachos and cheese, hot dogs, chili, chicken fingers, popcorn, sandwiches, and drinks on tap. There was even a waiter who would take our order and bring us whatever we wished. I had never gone to sporting events in this style. "So this is how the rich people live!" I remarked to the boys.

I sat in a front row seat behind a glass window, looking out onto the bright green playing field. I usually liked to sit close to the action on the field, but in this case, I didn't mind. Once the game started, everyone in the booth settled into their seats and watched the "Big Unit," Randy Johnson, throw the first pitch. I just knew I was going to have a great time.

I was hungry and thirsty, and all the food smelled so tempting, but I didn't order anything. I didn't bring much money with me, and I hated paying five or six dollars for a coke and even more for hot dogs or chicken fingers that I could buy outside the park for a dollar or two.

I kept thinking of what else I could buy after the game. I could get a steak dinner for the same money I would spend on just a few snacks. To curb my hunger, I always brought a small treat, such as a bag of M&Ms, in my pocket. As the game went on, I pulled out some candy whenever I felt hungry. Watching all the other people around me enjoy excellent food was tough, but I could not bring myself to pay all that money at the game.

It was a close game, and around the seventh inning, the waiter came over to me and asked whether I may want anything.

"I'm about to begin cleaning up, and this is the last call for food or drinks," he warned me.

The food looked and smelled so good, and I was starting to get hungry now, so I decided I would give in and get something.

"How much is it for a hot dog and a Coke?" I asked.

"Why sir, none of this food costs anything. It all comes with the suite. You have been missing out on some excellent stuff," he answered.

I couldn't believe my ears. I could have been eating all this time for free. I made up for a lost time. Nothing ever tastes as good as free food. I made sure that in that short period left, I would not feel cheated out of what I could be given.

Unfortunately, even with an ace pitcher throwing a solid game, the Astros lost., They lost the series and were eliminated from contention for the World Series that year. But on the way home, all I could remember was all the food that was just there for the taking. I realized then that maybe I was living my life that same way. God had given me so much! As I thought about my family, friends, job, and health, I realized I could just go on and on, counting all my blessings. God wants us to enjoy all of the wonders of this world. But how often do we settle for candy?

Consider your own life for a minute. Do you find yourself worried and upset all of the time? Are you missing out on the real joys and happiness that God has provided for you? Think of just the "little" things: a great meal, a quiet night with those who love you, a movie or television show that you look forward to, or maybe just another weekend coming up. How much do we just take for granted, when we realize how many others in this world can't even imagine what a life such as ours would be like?

We should be thankful each morning that we can wake up without pain or hunger and be with others doing something we enjoy all day.

Once God experimented. He chose an average man who wasn't doing well and made a deal with him.

"I tell you what," He said. "Give me your life. You aren't doing very well with it yourself. What do you have to lose? Turn your life over to me, and let's see what will happen."

The man decided he might as well. Pleased, very happy, and made terrible decisions. Now he wasn't doing very well and wasn't getting anywhere anyway.

"Okay, God," the man replied. "I'll take you up on this deal. Here, I'm just going to give my life over to you. You take charge and direct me from here on in."

Soon things began to turn around for the man. His marriage was working out much better than it ever had. God told him not to get discouraged when his job was getting to him. Sure enough, soon, he was offered a job that he had wanted. Taking a new position meant relocating, and after several months of waiting, his house did sell, and he found a much better one in his new city.

Other things also began to change for him. He now felt respected and appreciated in his new work. Without all of the hassle and stress of his old position, he loved getting up every morning and going to work. His daughter and his granddaughter moved in with him and his wife, and his son was now only two hours away. Financially he was better off than ever, and his health had improved; he felt great.

With God directing his life, he found three big keys to finding joy at work; first of all, find something you enjoy doing. Secondly, make sure the job aligns with your skill set. And finally, do something that can make a difference in other people's lives. God had blessed him with all three.

If God gave you everything you wanted, would you always find true joy and happiness? I wondered this since I was the man who gave my life to God. I can tell you this. Even with everything I could have ever asked for, I often seek peace and satisfaction. I guess that's part of being a sinful human being. If our lives were perfect, always happy, and without worry, we wouldn't need a heavier savior to bring us eternal peace and salvation.

QUESTION TO CONSIDER:

How much of life's exquisite pleasures are you missing out on because you are caught up in worry and anxiety?

God, you've created a wonderful world for us--may we treat each day as a special gift from You. Amen.

THE CADILLAC

Frank Angello always wanted a Cadillac. Not just any Cadillac, but a big, long, sleek Cadillac, with large fins in the back. Maybe it was because he was a tiny man, but he had dreamt of this big car all his life. But Frank was just a blue-collar worker in a factory and could never afford such a car. Besides, he had a wife and four kids to support, so he settled for his tiny little economy car.

Frank's children went to college and began their own families as time passed. Meanwhile Frank's hard work and dedication to his company paid off, and he was promoted several times. Finally, after his last promotion, Frank had the income to buy his dream car. He was so proud that day when he drove that shiny, black Cadillac onto his driveway. After years of hard work, long hours, and many sacrifices, it was his time to fulfill a lifelong dream.

Now I know that we all must be careful about judging other people. Outward appearances can be deceiving, and we can't look into someone's heart. But, there it was. Every Sunday, as our family and neighbors would get ready for church, rushing out the front door late, we would all see Frank. He would be out on his driveway, wearing work pants and a white t-shirt, washing, waxing, and shining that gigantic car. It just seemed to all of us, because it was Sunday morning, that Frank was worshipping his god out there. For him, washrags, soapy suds, and a plastic bucket were the means of worship. When he finished,d and that car gleaned in the noon sun; Frank would stand there for a while and bask in the glow of that magnificent sight.

A few years later, Frank passed away in his sleep. Rumor had it that he had requested in his will to be buried in that car. His friends said they could see him, with a big cigar in his mouth and a proud smile, saying," What a way to go!"

I don't think we have to worry about worshipping a golden calf or statue. But many other "things" become very important to us in our lives. We are constantly bombarded with me- media's concepts of what success and natural living are. All of us have our "Cadillacs" that we covet and desire.

In the Bible, the first commandment is, "You should have no other gods." In Luther's small catechism, we are told to "fear, love, and trust in God above all things." I know in my life, each day, I find myself putting God in the background as I give my attention to so many earthly things. I'm sure we could all make a long list of things we put ahead of God. Money, popularity, comfort, respect, admiration, success at work, a loving spouse and family, power, influence, nice clothes, good health, and so on. We forget about God and focus only on our selfish wants and needs all the time. Maybe we go to church each Sunday and convince ourselves how commendable this is, but that is only one hour out of a week.

Turning our attention to God instead of our selfish wants is a tremendous challenge for us. We must pray often and ask The Holy Spirit to fill our hearts with love toward God throughout the day. Remember, in the final moment of our lives, the only thing that will matter is our acceptance of God's forgiveness of our sins through Jesus.

God created a wonderful world with many blessings for us to share and enjoy. But we must be careful to keep everything in the proper perspective. God must come first. As they say, we've never seen a hearse pulling a U-Haul. You can't take anything with you.

QUESTION TO CONSIDER:

Think of a time when you gave in to society's message that you always need the newest and improved new model. Did it bring you the joy you thought it would, or did you start waiting for the next new model?

God, keep us from getting caught up in the material world and help us to focus on what is essential in our lives. Amen.

MOTIVATION 2

Once, a young man was trying to scratch out a living selling vacuum cleaners. He went from house to house, never knowing who would be on the other side of the door or what kind of situation he would find himself in when he knocked. One day when he rang the doorbell, a beautiful young lady wearing a very revealing outfit opened the door. She smiled and invited him in when he told her that his vacuum cleaner was the best money could buy and that he would be glad to demonstrate it on one of her carpets. Once in the living room, he started looking for a plug to start his vacuum.

"Oh no, I would much rather have you clean the carpet in my bedroom," the woman requested. "That would show me how well your machine works."

At first, the young man felt a little funny about going into the bedroom with this gorgeous woman, but then he figured that if it got him a sale, he would do just as she wished.

Once inside the bedroom, he plugged in the vacuum cleaner and started to put it to the test. Just then, he heard a noise in the front room.

"What's that noise?" he asked.

"Oh no, that must be my husband coming home early. I didn't expect him for another several hours. He's a professional wrestler, and he is always very jealous."

The salesman immediately realized he was in the wrong place at the wrong time. He didn't know if the short-tempered giant would even give him time to explain what he was doing.

"Don't panic, ma'am. I'll go through the back door before he comes here."

The young lady looked alarmed. "But this house doesn't have a back door."

As the salesman looked out of the bedroom door and saw that the lady's husband was getting closer to them, he yelled to the woman," Okay then, where would you like one?"

QUESTION TO CONSIDER:

Do we ever sell ourselves short on what we can accomplish? Sometimes only when we have no other choice do we apply ourselves.

105

TELL YOUR STORY

Have you ever seen people who stand by the side of the road at a busy intersection and hold up a sign that tells us to repent of their evil ways and follow Jesus? I admire these individuals' faith and dedication, but I wonder how effective their message is to passers-by.

I believe that if we want to effectively bring the message of salvation to others, we must first build relationships and then tell our own stories. People don't care how much we know until they know how much we care. We must be genuine to them and show them that we do care about them.

A friend of mine had the unenviable job of raising money for a Lutheran high school. Many people were wealthy enough to give considerable sums to his school in the town where he lived. But how could he motivate them to want to provide?

His plan was straightforward. He would take them out to lunch in- dividually, and they would get to know each other. He would do this often and continue building a solid relationship with them. He wouldn't start by asking them for money but instead concentrate on getting to know them. It might take him years to build such a relationship, but once others saw that he cared about them and had a strong passion for the school's ministry, they wanted to help his cause.

The same model is necessary if we want to be effective witnesses to Christ. If someone doesn't know you or anything about you, they will not tend to want to listen to your message. But the message of salvation is too important. People would rather see a sermon than hear one. If we can show the world that we preach love, kindness, and a willingness to help, then we can begin to open their hearts to the Holy Spirit, and they can experience the absolute joy of life. Suddenly things can start to make sense, and they can find a purpose and direction in their lives. But this newfound joy and happiness in this world is only a byproduct of a much more important cause. They can spend all eternity in Heaven. What could mean more than that?

QUESTION TO CONSIDER:

Have you ever found in your life that building genuine, lasting relationships with others has blessed you in many ways?

God, you've given us others to turn to in times of trouble and need. May we use the gift of friendship to help us each step in our daily journeys through rocky times. Amen.

NO FAILURES.

Have you ever really wanted something, only to be disappointed when it didn't happen for you? When this does happen, we can get very emotional. What is wrong with us? Why am I such a loser? I was cheated. I should have gotten that job! Life is not fair. Why did God not answer my prayers? Now I have let everyone down, especially my family and friends. It's all my fault. I did not do enough, or I'm just not good enough. I just want to give up and quit. What is the sense of keeping trying when I just don't have what it takes to be a success? I look around me and see many others doing better than I am. I have been such a failure.

I'm sure that there were times in our lives when we felt like this. There was something that we wanted, and we prayed that God would bless us with it. When it didn't happen, we were heartbroken. We couldn't understand why God let us be so disappointed when we felt we deserved it.

It was time. An opening in the office had come up, and today the boss was going to announce who would receive the promotion. There was a lot at stake-money, prestige, structure, and success. Jim had worked hard for so long and was always loyal to the company. Bob was also up for the promotion and wanted it. Late in the afternoon, the announcement came. Neither Jim nor Bob had been chosen.

Jim was very bitter and angry when he heard the news. He felt that when he told his wife and family, they would think he was a failure. But when Jim talked to Bob about the bad news, he was shocked at Bob's outlook. "Jim," Bob said, " I tried my best and wanted the promotion, but I can accept the reality that God just has another plan for me in the future."

Looking at things this way did make Jim feel better. He didn't fail or lose. God just had another plan for him. He just had to understand that this was just not his time.

Years later, when Jim and Bob met at a party, they both looked back on that incident and now understood why

God didn't make it happen. Both men went on to find much greater success than they would have had if they had been promoted then.

Whenever we don't get what we want in life, we don't have to look at it as failure or our shortcomings. God has a different time and place for us in His plans.

If this has ever sounded like you, here's a secret. Here's a way to never feel like a failure when things don't go your way. I will tell you how you can live in peace and contentment and stop blaming yourself and others for losseslures and disappointments. Does that sound good to you? Okay, here's my personal advice:

PUT THE BURDEN ON GOD. That's right. Do your best, try your hardest, and then, if something doesn't work out, put it on, God. God is in charge of the world and everything in it. If it was not His will for something to happen, then accept His plan for your life.

God, I pray to you that I get this promotion. I have done my part. I have worked hard and done my best. Now it's on you. If I don't get the raise, it simply was not your plan for my life. Nobody failed or came up short---this is what You have decided for my life. Besides, you know best anyway. Your plan will be better than anything I could have wished and dreamt of. I will turn to the next page of my life and see what you have in store for me. I don't fail--I try my best and leave it all up to you. I am now at peace in my life. I now realize more than ever that we only have one life to live. We must make the most of it and cherish every moment we have.

QUESTION TO CONSIDER:

Think of a time when you didn't get what you wanted and prayed for. Later did you see that God had a better plan for you?

God, you know us and know what is best for us. Help us to trust You to follow the plans. You have for us so that we may prosper and find true joy and peace in our lives. Amen.

We can find many things in our lives that bring out our passion and excitement. The promise of eternal salvation in heaven should bring peace and comfort and certainly mean so much to us that we want to share the message of Jesus saving us to all the world. God bless you!